Caterham

in old picture postcards

by
Jean Tooke (text)
and
Roger Packham (postcards)

With very best wishes from
Jean Tooke (née Sheppard)

European Library – Zaltbommel/Netherlands

Acknowledgements
To Margaret Duck for proof-reading the text.
To Caterham residents for identifying places and checking dates.

Sixth edition: 1988

GB   ISBN 90 288 3337 4 / CIP

INTRODUCTION

In 1905, Alec Braid, newspaper editor, printer and stationer, advertised 150 different picture postcards for sale, the majority being local views taken with his own camera. His April list of 13 new cards included 'Caterham Valley Evening Express Train' (37) and 'Croydon Road and Beechlands' (58). From 1898, when he became editor of the 'Caterham Free Press', renamed 'Caterham Weekly Press' in 1901, until his appointment as Photographic Manager of the 'Daily Graphic' in 1910, he recorded every aspect of Caterham life.

The official Guards' Depot photographers, Harry Fenton Runicles (H. Fenton) working from 1887 until his death in 1913 and George and Herbert Bunce (Bunce Bros.) from 1902 until their retirement over fifty years later, also produced local postcards. Upper Caterham postmaster, Henry Grinstead and stationers T.W. Relfe, L. Ledger and the Fancy Stores published their own series.

These local photographers presented Caterham, 18 miles from London, as a small prosperous Surrey town set amid splendid North Downs scenery. Yet in 1851 its population had only totalled 487, centred on the village on the Hill. Ten years later the increased population of 815 reflected the first of three major events which would completely transform the town's character. In 1856 the South-Eastern Railway extended the line from Caterham Junction (Purley) primarily to transport stone from Godstone Hill quarries. The by-product was the development of Caterham Valley. Desirable mansions were sold in the beautiful Harestone Valley with free first class annual season tickets for purchasers.

By 1871, Upper Caterham had begun to change dramatically. The opening of the Metropolitan Asylum (St. Lawrence's Hospital) in 1870 for the mentally sub-normal from London workhouses had increased the population to 3,577. Four years later the War Office purchased land adjoining the Asylum to transfer the Guards' Recruiting Depot from Warley, Essex. In the 1881 Census returns 6,258 inhabitants were enumerated — 1,781 on the Hill, 1,813 in the Valley, 503 stationed in the Depot and 2,161 living in the Asylum. During the next fifty years, the population increased steadily to 14,880 in 1931.

Caterham had grown from a self-contained village to a small town, whose residents worked locally in the new institutions or commuted by rail to Croydon or the City to businesses often connected with the profitable imperial trade. The High Street houses were converted to shops serving Asylum staff and Army personnel. In contrast the Valley shopping centre was primarily built for affluent customers living in their well-staffed mansions. This prosperous middle-class required and subscribed to new facilities. Imposing churches were built. St. Mary's Church was dedicated in 1866, the Congregational Church in 1875, the Sacred Heart Roman Catholic Church in 1881, St. John's Church in 1882 and the Wesleyan Chapel opposite the Guards' Depot in 1908.

Churchmen of all denominations attended the traditional ratepayers Vestry, chaired by the Rector but replaced by an elected Parish Council in 1895. Problems arose, for Caterham, one of 14 parishes in the Godstone Union, paid one third of the rates, but did not have a third of the representatives. Its application to become an Urban District Council was granted in 1899. Godstone claimed compensation. The dispute was finally settled in Caterham's favour in 1904 by the House of Lords in the celebrated 'Caterham-Godstone Adjustment case'. William Garland Soper, who led the fight for independence, was co-opted first Chairman of Caterham Urban District Council.

The Vestry, Parish Council and Urban District Council conscientiously improved amenities. The Gas Company was incorporated in 1869, the Spring Water Company in 1872 and the Electric Urban Supply Company in 1903. In 1904, an ambitious main drainage scheme planned by Henry Martin, Caterham Urban District Council's first surveyor, was started. Queen's Park was laid out in 1900 and Timber Hill purchased the same year.

Education was the parish's responsibility from 1870 to 1901. Elementary schools were opened on the Hill and in the Valley in 1872 by the elected School Board. Its chairman, William Soper and other congregationalists were instrumental in the 'School for the Sons of Congregational Ministers' (Caterham School) moving to Harestone Valley in 1884. Day boys were later admitted, some with Surrey County Council scholarships.

'Harestone', William Soper's home, was the venue for garden parties in aid of the Cottage Hospital, opened by H.R.H. Princess Christian in 1903. These wealthy residents ensured the success of local organisations by attending committees, donating prizes, heading subscription lists and persuading well-known people to address meetings and open bazaars. St. John's Ambulance Brigade, Caterham Institute, the Village Club, Band of Hope, Horticultural Society, Fanciers' Club, the United Silver Band, the Cycling, Cricket, Football, Hockey, Bowls and Rifle Clubs all benefited from their patronage.

Their concern extended to the Guards' Depot by supporting the Soldiers' Home built in 1898 as an off-duty social centre. However, after 15,000 patriotic recruits descended on Caterham in 1915 during the First World War, all available halls were used, manned by lady volunteers who provided meals and helped the men write letters and cards home.

The soldiers' choice of postcards were Depot scenes — the Parade Ground or Guards' Chapel. Domestic servants in the large residences also sent their families cards, usually to confirm their safe arrival. Views of War Coppice were popular with visitors to the Surrey Hills. Albums were filled by collectors, for 1900-1930 was the golden age of postcard collecting. The Acme Photo Works, Upper Caterham, printed no less than 20 million cards on their Graber machine between 1926 and 1930.

We are indebted to a modern collector, Roger Packham, for the postcards in this volume chosen from his splendid local history collection and to Ann Walmsley for the cover postcard of the Old Rectory.

Jean Tooke

1. St. Lawrence's Church, the tiny Norman church built in 1095 and situated at the top of Church Hill, is one of the oldest churches in Surrey. Although small, it was quite adequate for the North Downs village whose population in 1851 was only 487. However, when the railway was extended to Caterham in 1856, land was sold for building. Large mansions appeared on the Hill and in the Valley, so a more substantial church, suitable for a larger and more affluent population, was considered necessary. After St. Mary's Church was opened in 1866, the font was removed to St. John's Church, Caterham Valley and the church was little used except for Sunday school activities. In 1927 it was restored and reconsecrated.

St. Mary's, Upper Caterham.

Copyright Fenton Caterham

2. St. Mary's Church, opened in 1866, was built on land opposite the old church at a cost of £2,200. It was originally planned to demolish St. Lawrence's Church, using the stone for building the new church, but the Bishop of Winchester intervened. In 1866 only a chancel and nave were built with seating for 350 worshippers. By 1883, this was inadequate so £3,600 was raised to build the south aisle, south chancel and the tower topped by the 126 ft. spire, a local landmark. The choir vestry was added in 1899 and the north aisle in 1912. This view of the south side is now obscured by the addition of the church hall erected in 1970.

Caterham. Top of Waller Lane. A.D.S.

3. The Dene, opened in 1906, was a purpose-built boys' preparatory school, standing in 1½ acres at the corner of Church Road and Waller Lane opposite Queen's Park. The school, founded in 1873, had been transferred from Underwood Road, Harestone Valley. The centrally heated buildings included a 54 ft. school room, gymnasium, carpenter's shop and a bicycle house. It is now a hospital. Behind the school in Waller Lane is 'Fawsley', owned by Henry Martin, appointed Caterham Urban District Council's first surveyor in 1899 and who played an important part in Caterham's development. 'No cycling. This hill is dangerous,' states the notice at the top of Waller Lane, the road leading down to Caterham Valley. The signpost directs carriages along Church Road.

WHYTELEAFE ROAD, CATERHAM.

4. Whyteleafe Road, leading from Church Road, was bordered by spacious Victorian and Edwardian houses. This lodge, still standing, was at the entrance to 'Essendene'. The estate extended to Burntwood Lane to the north and down the hill to the Stafford Road estates to the east. Fashionable garden parties and local shows were held in the attractive grounds.

CATERHAM·FLOWER·SHOW·1907·AFB

5. The Flower Show held at 'Essendene', Whyteleafe Road on 24th July 1907, according to the 'Caterham Free Press', had a 'wealth of excellent exhibits, sweet peas taking the foremost place, closely followed by strawberries, while the vegetables were the best this season at any local exhibition'. A judge commented that 'Caterham gardeners have come in trumps on the chalk'. Professional gardeners from the large houses, cottagers and ladies of the district competed in over 100 classes for the Challenge cups and other prizes. Splendid set pieces were displayed by local nurserymen, Rayner Hill from the Valley and Frank Brazier on the Hill. Robert Vigar, the Townend blacksmith, exhibited horticultural and agricultural implements. Ices and teas were sold by Mr. Chalmers of the 'Blacksmiths Arms', while the Caterham Valley Reed and Brass Band played selections during the afternoon and evening.

Caterham. Queen's Park.

The seats under the pavilion could tell a few tales.

6. Queen's Park was opened on 23rd May 1900. The 18 acres had been purchased by the Parish Council for £1,800 in 1898 to commemorate Queen Victoria's Diamond Jubilee in 1897. This attractive pavilion and a smaller sports pavilion, costing together £900, were donated by Harry Lloyd of 'Woodlands', Stanstead Road and William Garland Soper of 'Harestone', the first Caterham Urban District Council Chairman. After the opening ceremony, many attractions were arranged — fancy bicycle and ladies' tortoise races, a tug of war, military and gymnastic displays and exhibition drills by the Fire Brigade, culminating in an evening firework display and torchlight procession down Church Hill to the fountain in the Square.

7. The Queen's Park drinking fountain, donated by Frederick White of 'Portley' is seen in front of the newly built houses in Queen's Park Road. Between the trees is the Borer Ambulance Station, housing the hand-drawn ambulance. This memorial to Harry Borer, a Caterham St. John's Ambulance Brigade member, who died in Portland, South Africa in June 1900 during the Boer War, was opened on 24th June 1902. The site was chosen as Queen's Park was used for sports fixtures. Football and cricket matches were played several times a week while the Bowls Club was founded nine years later in June, 1911.

The Rectory, Caterham.

8. The Rectory was originally a small timber framed house thought to have been built in the 16th century. Later additions were made in the 18th and 19th centuries by successive rectors. A modern rectory was built in the grounds in 1955. The building was carefully and sympathetically restored in 1984 by local builders W. & R. Buxton Ltd. who now use it for their offices.

Caterham : The Old Village

9. These picturesque High Street cottages were opposite the Rectory. Although weatherboarded 'Rectory Cottages' and 'Clematis Cottage' next door have been replaced by a small housing development, number 84, shown on the 1736 Rowed Map, is still occupied. The branches of the massive cedar tree, which in 1909 stood inside the Rectory garden, are overhanging the road. This view of 'The Old Village' was popular with Edwardian postcard publishers. Emma Vigar, daughter of the Townend blacksmith, sent this card to a friend in Great Yarmouth.

10. T.W. Relfe, the High Street newsagent next to the 'Royal Oak', published this postcard in 1929. Posing for the photograph, taken by Frith's of Reigate, is perhaps a newsboy with his bicycle propped up against the shop window. Beyond Paine's the bootmaker and Leiston's hairdressing establishment are the three 18th century 'Roffey Cottages', demolished in 1964. On the right are 69-75 High Street, then private houses with their iron railings bordering the road before the pavement was added and the High Street widened.

HIGH ST UPPER CATERHAM.

11. 'Box Cottage' with its picturesque thatched roof was replaced by modern shops in 1964, despite efforts to make it a listed building. The roof was not without hazard, as several times it caught fire, although a fireman lived there! Behind the hedge on the right was the Rectory field, the Park Football team's home ground. In the distance is the 'Blacksmiths Arms' opened in 1820, a fully licensed public house, while the 'King and Queen' directly opposite, hidden by the house on the left, had been a beer house since 1845.

'SPORTS' CATERHAM. Aug 4. 13. W.F.W.No. 11.

12. The 'Village Sports' held on August Bank Holiday Monday 1913 was organised by the Cycling and Athletic Club in aid of the Cottage Hospital. The weather, according to the 'Caterham Weekly Press' 'took an unfavourable turn in the afternoon'. Twenty-five events were arranged including amusing novelty races – cycle musical chairs, a cigarette race and apple diving. Champion cyclist was Harry Jones, the Valley fishmonger's son. Prizes were donated by local residents and tradesmen including the Cycling Club President Henry Poland of 'Greenlands' Buxton Lane and Messrs. Page & Overton, the brewery owning the 'King and Queen', the 'Royal Oak' and 'The Greyhound' in the Valley.

13. The Caterham United Silver Band, amalgamated in 1908 from the Caterham Valley Reed and Brass Band and the Caterham Brass Band, played a selection of music at the 1913 Bank Holiday Sports. This photograph was taken in June 1911 after the Denton Challenge Cup was won at the Southern Counties Amateur Band Concert on Whit-Monday. The bandmaster Charles Hunt is sitting in the centre of the front row behind the cup. The bandsmen, wearing their new red uniforms, are holding their silver instruments costing 300 guineas, raised by organising concerts and by public subscription to the 'New Instruments Fund'.

HIGH STREET, CATERHAM.

14. In this High Street view, looking towards the 'King and Queen', the weatherboarded house on the left has been replaced by shops next to the Community Centre but the Soldiers' Home on the right is still standing. Purpose-built with money raised by local churchmen of all denominations, it provided recruits at the Guards' Depot with a 'home from home' where meals and non-alcoholic drinks could be obtained. Field Marshall Lord Roberts, after the opening ceremony in October 1898, addressed the crowded street from the first floor balcony. Adjoining it was the Caterham Urban District Council Fire Engine House with the bell turret, housing the horse-drawn Merryweather manual fire engine bought in 1889. The extension was added in 1900 for the fire escape.

15. Caterham Fire Brigade is standing by the side of its handcart after winning the Challenge cup at one of the many local or national competitions held to encourage smartness and efficiency. On one notable occasion, Caterham outdistanced the better equipped London Brigades at uphill manoeuvres. The Fire Brigade gave Exhibition drills at local shows and took part in Friendly Society processions. The firemen worked part-time; their efficient and enterprising captain, Robert Vigar, on the right, was the blacksmith at Townend Forge. Appointed in 1889, when the Brigade was established, he held the position until his death in 1923.

HIGH STREET, CATERHAM.

16. Townend Forge and ironmonger's shop built by Robert Vigar in 1884 opposite the 'Golden Lion' was conveniently near the Fire Engine House. A successful blacksmith, first-prize winner for shoeing hunters at the Royal Agricultural Show in Carlisle in 1902, membership of the Farriers company was conferred on him at their Annual Banquet on 10th November. Outside the shop are tin baths, while wheelbarrows and a sundial are for sale outside the forge. On the right, next to the Fire Engine House, is the Infants' Board School, built in 1872.

The Causeway. Upper-Caterham

17. This view of the Causeway (now Town End), looking towards the 'Golden Lion' and the Infants' Board School, shows Huggetts shoe shop established in 1857 and still owned by the same family. 'Myrtle Cottages', the eight small terraced houses, ending with a sweet shop converted from the front room, have been demolished to make way for the Raglan Precinct.

Chaldon Road, Caterham-on-the-Hill.

T.S.
CTHM. 17.

18. Chaldon Road was formerly called Reigate Road. The trees on the right were outside the Board School. On the left, next to the 'Golden Lion', were 'Woodlands Cottages', listed in the 1871 census. These typical terraced houses, built on the Hill in the 1870's for the Metropolitan Asylum workers, were on the site of the Raglan Precinct.

Chaldon Rd. Caterham. 2

19. The Board School (now Hillcroft) was opened in 1872 by the Caterham School Board, elected by the local ratepayers after the 1871 Education Act became law. The separate Boys', Girls' and Infants' Schools replaced the small National School founded by Thomas Clarke, lord of the manor, in 1804. The stone drinking fountain stood at the intersection of Chaldon Road and Westway. Advertisements for Spratts biscuits and chicken meal, on the left, were fixed on the side wall of Coulings, an old established corn and seed merchants, whose motor driven mill for grinding animal feed was housed in the barn at the rear. The business was closed for redevelopment in 1970.

CHALDON ROAD, CATERHAM.

20. The view from the corner of London Road and Chaldon Road of the solidly constructed houses built before the First World War, between Park Road and Court Road has changed little, although many houses have been modernised. However, due to nearby supermarkets, the small neighbourhood shops have altered. The tobacconist on the right has been converted to a private house, the butcher's to 'Video Hire' while the hairdresser on the left, symbolised by the barber's pole outside, is now a Bathroom Centre.

The Clifton, Upper Caterham, Surrey.
Proprietor · W. Smith.

21. The 'Clifton Arms' was one of eight public houses on the Hill, five of them opened at the time the Metropolitan Asylum was built. This advertising card, printed in 1907, would have been given to the regular clientele of tradesmen, army personnel, asylum attendants and asylum visitors. Secretaries of football and cricket clubs would have received a card to encourage them to book lunches, dinners and smoking concerts. The fine array of handpumps makes an impressive display.

Coulsdon Road. 2.

22. The 'Tally Ho' Livery and Bait stables were situated at the junction of Coulsdon Road and Banstead Road. 'Motors For Hire' is advertised on the board as well as 'Open and Closed Carriages', although only horses and carts can be seen, their owners doubtless enjoying a drink in the 'Tally Ho' public house. The terraced cottages are no longer there except for the shop adjoining St. Mary's Mission Hall with its patterned tiled roof. This was opened in 1884 on land belonging to Jeremiah Long of 'Arthur's Seat', White Hill to serve the new, growing population near the Guards' Depot. The Guards' Chapel roof can be seen behind the cottages.

St. Michael's Road, Caterham.

23. St. Michael's Road was part of a footpath from Chaldon across Caterham Common, which continued along Addison Road. The narrow white path is now between houses in Banstead Road. St. Paul's Church and Le Personne Homes were erected on the large field on the right. The houses beyond the field are nos. 20 and 22 Le Personne Road. Addison Road houses can be seen behind the trees on the left.

"On Parade," Guard's Depot, Caterham."

24. The Guards' Depot was opened in 1877 as the Recruiting Depot for the Grenadier, Coldstream and Scots Guards. The original barrack blocks, enlarged, but still in use, were built for 500 men. The Officers' Mess also built in 1877, can be seen behind the Parade Ground. The cost of building St. Michael's Church, opened in 1886, was financed by public subscription. Seating 650 men, it was used for Anglican, Roman Catholic and Nonconformist worship. The new recruits are seen learning their drill, although a few are in uniform.

Caterham. Guard's Depot. The Gymnasium.

25. Gymnastics played an important part in the recruits' two month training programme with its emphasis on physical fitness. Outside drills were held on the Parade Ground three times a day and under cover in the Drill Sheds in bad weather. The football and cricket teams played local clubs. Gymnastic demonstrations, Swedish drill displays, sword and bayonet exercises were presented at local functions or at the Depot Open Days or its annual Horticultural Show. The Regimental Bands were also a popular attraction at these events or at concerts given in the Public Hall in Godstone Road.

CATERHAM GUARDS' DEPÔT. THE COOK HOUSE.

26. The single storey Cookhouse was situated between Albermarle and Cambridge barrack blocks. Catering was important as many recruits arrived undernourished and unfit. The container, held by the cook second on the left, was destined for York block. Behind the cooks, a painter can be seen, as building operations were carried on continuously. Although such work was done by army personnel, local firms would also be invited to submit tenders for specific jobs.

Caterham. Guard's Depot.
Coffee-Bar.

27. The Coffee-Bar does not look well patronised, although every effort was made by the military authorities to keep the men sober off-duty. With twelve public houses within walking distance, the military pickets were a familiar sight on Friday and Saturday nights. Games rooms and a recreation pavilion were built where weekly concerts and entertainments would be arranged by the N.C.O.'s, to which Caterham residents would be invited, the profits donated to an army or local charity such as the Soldiers' Home in the High Street or the Cottage Hospital.

The Asylum" Caterham.

Fenton.

28. The Metropolitan Asylum opened in 1870 as a result of the 1867 Metropolitan Poor Act. By 1881 it housed over 2,000 staff and patients, most of them born in the London area. This was one third of Caterham's population. The character of the Hill changed completely. Not only did the site occupy 154 acres, but fields and common land were used for access roads, such as Coulsdon Road and Westway, and for houses built along these roads for the non-resident staff and ancillary workers. New shops were opened and businesses started.

COULSDON RD CATERHAM.   D.F.C°

29. Coulsdon Road 1904, showing some soldiers marching towards the entrance to the Metropolitan Asylum where a postman has just made his collection. Opposite can be seen the sign for 'The Asylum Tavern' which was built at the corner of Asylum Road to provide refreshment for the 2,000 building labourers. When the Asylum was completed in 1870, it was patronised by the residential and non-residential staff. The decision to transfer the Guards' Depot to Caterham in 1877 ensured its survival. Since then, it has been renamed 'The Caterham Arms'.

Asylum Road, Upper Caterham.

30. Asylum Road (now Westway), as its name implies, was the short cut from the High Street to the Asylum main gates over Caterham Common. Looking towards the Common, on the right, were houses built for private occupation, like Armboth House, built in 1891, later converted to Lambirth's Stores. When shops were built opposite in 1906, George and Henry Bunce, sons of an Asylum tailor, opened the Langdale Photographic Studios. They specialised in photographing events at the Guards Depot – group photographs of the training squads to large company groups which often included senior army generals or members of the royal family. In addition they photographed many local occasions or views which had a ready sale when reproduced as postcards.

On Caterham Common

31. This delightful Edwardian photograph was taken on Caterham Common near the junction of Asylum Road and Chaldon Road. The children may have been returning home from school, as the Board School is beyond the trees on the right. The roof with the bell turret is St. Mary's Parish Hall, opened on 8th October 1900 on the site of Hillcroft School Dining Hall. This card was sent to Mrs. Edwards at 'Beechlands Lodge', Stafford Road with the remark 'I think Maggie has come out the best, don't you.'

32. Church Hill, originally the carriage drive to Caterham Court by St. Lawrence's Church, divided Caterham into two communities – the old village of Upper Caterham and the newly developed Caterham Valley. Looking down the hill towards the valley, the Woldingham hills can be seen in the distance. 'Tryon House', on the left, sometimes called 'Swiss Cottage', stood on the site of a hollowed out chalk pit. The lamp-post marks the start of Jacob's Ladder and further down the hill is the entrance to 'Mountside'.

33. Jacob's Ladder, a shortcut from the Hill to Harestone Valley, was part of a footpath leading to Tupwood from Waller Lane via The Hill, Colbourn Avenue and Grange Road. The 167 steps were fenced, as 'Mountside' grounds were on the right of this photograph and 'Fairbank' in Harestone Valley on the left. The level stretch towards the top of the steps was part of the original drive from the Valley to Caterham Court before it was diverted.

Caterham, Waller Lane.

34. Waller Lane was the old road leading from the village to the Valley 300 feet below. It was preferred by many pedestrians even after Church Hill was made up in 1922. Cycling was forbidden and offenders were fined as it was considered dangerous for pedestrians. The gateway on the left is the side entrance to 'Rose Cottage', once the lodge to 'Sylva House'. The steps on the right led to the back entrance of 'Bishams', a large house, now demolished, which stood at the corner of Waller Lane and Church Hill. This postcard, in sepia, was published by Frith's of Reigate in 1905.

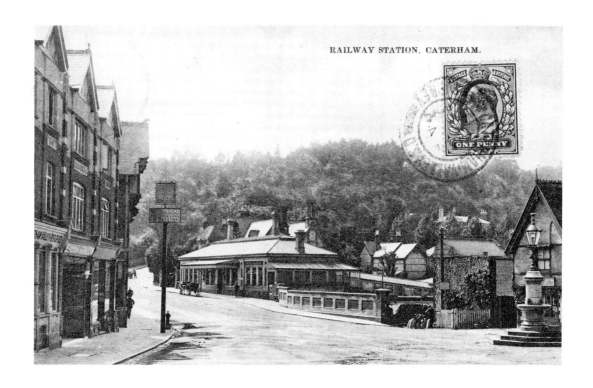

RAILWAY STATION, CATERHAM.

35. The Railway Station in the Square was rebuilt in 1900 after the single track from Purley had been doubled. Opened 44 years earlier in 1856, the railway was the principal factor in the Valley's development. In 1851, there were an inn, two isolated farms, and cottages near the chalkpits. By 1881 nearly 2,000 people lived in the fashionable Harestone Valley mansions and the smaller properties around Croydon Road. Behind the station are the roofs of 'The Priory', since demolished, its outbuildings and the adjoining Masonic Hall – originally the Congregational Chapel (now Stafford Hall). The house was occupied by William Garland Soper before he moved to 'Harestone'.

S 3499   CATERHAM STATION.

36. Caterham station is photographed from the original platform. The central platform and new tracks were laid between 1897 and 1900. As the time shown on the station clock is 6.05 pm, perhaps the party of young ladies was planning to catch the 6.10 pm train scheduled to arrive at London Bridge at 6.50 pm and Charing Cross at 7.06 pm. The annual season ticket to London in 1908 was £21 first class and £16.5s second class.

Caterham Valley. The Evening Express.
Braid's Series. *Have just got home not* 3/2/1900/. *Did you get my letter late. ?*

37. 'The Evening Express' arriving at Caterham station, was photographed by Alec Braid in 1905. The signal box at the end of the platform was dismantled in 1985. On the right is the 110 foot brick chimney constructed by the Urban Electric Supply Company for their steam boiler. This chimney caused a certain amount of controversy when the generating station was opened in the Croydon Road opposite the 'Commonwealth Tavern' in 1903.

38. The residential 'Railway Hotel', opposite the station, was rebuilt in 1902. Its meeting rooms included one large enough for theatrical entertainments. Behind were tea gardens popular with cyclists and day trippers. On Saturday, 23rd May 1903, tea was provided for four London cycling clubs. Sixty staff from the 'Financial Times' who had walked to Blindley Heath and back, not only had tea, but an evening concert and dance on the lawn. On the left is Worlds Stores with wicker chairs suspended from the top of its window, while on the right, Lovegrove and Letch have panama hats hanging by the door. The Surrey Hills Estate Agency above was opened before 1867 to sell the new Valley properties.

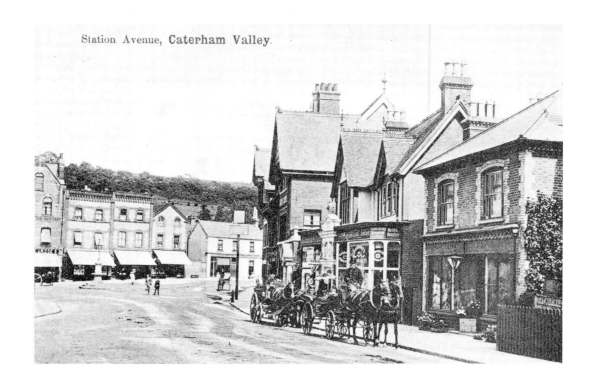

Station Avenue, Caterham Valley.

39. In Station Avenue was Rayner Hill's nursery which covered the present Valley car park and the site of the present Post Office, the third to be situated in the Square. The original Post Office was in the two-storey building seen behind the Railway Hotel sign, at the corner of Timber Hill. In 1905, it was occupied by Bromley Hall, corn and seed merchants. Next to Rayner Hill, underneath the Surrey Hills Estate Agency, was Percy Broad's 'Model Bakery', advertising Cadbury's Chocolate on the windows, whose cakes won many prizes in national competitions. Outside are the smart carriages from the Harestone Valley mansions driven by uniformed coachmen.

40. The Old Surrey Hounds must have been a colourful sight when they met in the Square. The small boys and one girl are crowded on the drinking fountain steps. Presented by the London jeweller, Charles Asprey of 'Beechlands', Stafford Road in November 1890, the fountain has been transferred to White Knobs Recreation Ground. The 'Old Surrey Hounds', seen on the left, was destroyed by fire in the early hours of 2nd May 1916, causing £2,000 worth of damage. The staff escaped from the first floor by tying sheets to a bedstead, while the manager, Arthur Beard, had the presence of mind to throw down his cash box containing the weekend takings.

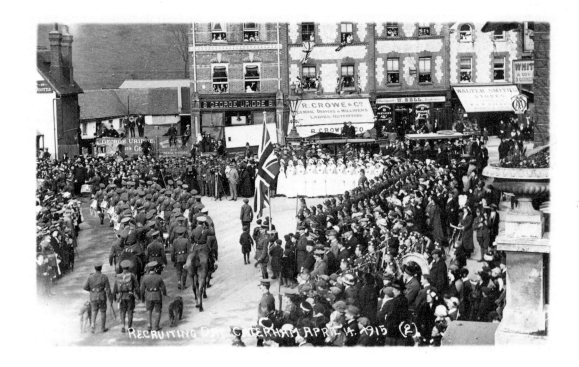

RECRUITING DAY CATERHAM APRIL 14. 1915. (R)

41. The Recruiting Parade, on Wednesday afternoon 15th April 1915, was held to encourage voluntary enlistment. Over 3,000 men took part from the Guards, Royal Fusiliers, the Public Schools Battalion, the Royal Sussex Regiment and the local Volunteers. Brig.-General R.H. Twigg, of the 119th Infantry Brigade, standing by the Union Jack, took the salute. Caterham Red Cross detachment under the command of Dr. Morgan Thomas can be seen in the Square. The procession, which included the Guards' Drum and Fife Band and the London Scottish Territorials Pipers started at the Depot and finished at Whyteleafe, where the children from the Council School sang the National Anthem.

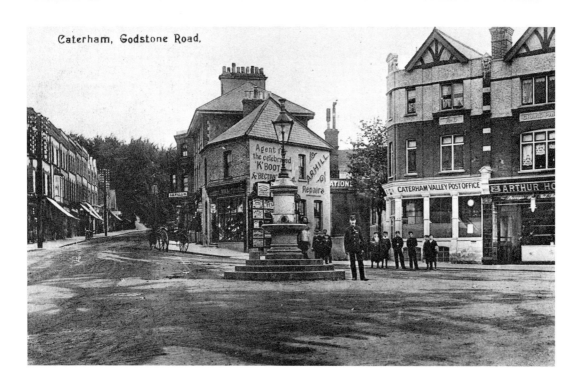

Caterham, Godstone Road.

42. Caterham Valley Post Office moved from the corner of Timber Hill Road in February 1904 to the Grand Parade, built in 1903. The telegraph boys can be seen in the background. There were four postal deliveries a day and one on Sundays. The Post Office, employing eight indoor staff and fourteen postmen, was open from 8 am to 8 pm on weekdays and for two hours on Sunday mornings. Allen Hill's boot and shoe shop, advertising 'K' boots, was on the other corner of Church Walk. Behind was the rear of Ledger's stationery and gift store. At the end of the Godstone Road row of shops on the left was St. John's School. The trees in the distance were on a small plantation on the corner of Godstone and Crescent roads.

Caterham Printing Works.

Godstone Road, Caterham Valley. 6140.

43. Godstone Road photographed in 1915 during the First World War. Cars were replacing carriages, so Kilby's, the Livery Stables by the station had opened a 'Garage and Motor Works' in the single storey building on the right, which later became a British Restaurant during the Second World War. St. John's School (now the Miller Centre), on the right, had moved to this site on 24th March 1884. The building was originally St. John's temporary church in Clareville Road. Not required when the new church opened in December 1882, the parish economically decided to use it as the church school, moving it to Godstone Road opposite the new church.

44. 'Surrey Hills Hydropathic and Turkish Baths establishment for Residents and Visitors' known as 'The Hydro' was opened in August 1898 by local ironmonger John Burford on 22 acres previously owned by William Gwynne, the proprietor of the Railway Hotel. Turkish, electric, sulphur and mustard baths were provided in Italian mosaic and marble bathrooms. The 21 bedrooms had uninterrupted hillside views. After John Burford's death, it was reopened in May 1903 as a branch of the Michigan based Battle Creek Sanitarium. The principles of a simple diet, fresh air and unrestricted clothing were considered revolutionary eighty years ago.

THE SANITARIUM CATERHAM, ENGLAND.

45. The Sanitarium buildings, photographed from the gardens, included double fronted 'Cambrian House' on the right and 1 and 2 'The Villas', two of six identical three-storey semi-detached houses, on the left. These two buildings were cleverly joined by an extension with its small tower adjoining 'The Villas'. By 1927 it was a private hotel, but on 6th March 1941, there was a disastrous fire caused by a cigarette spark igniting the carpet in the ground floor sun lounge. The proprietress and six guests were killed. The original 'Cambrian House' and the second floor bedrooms in the centre extension were destroyed.

3688. Tupwood, Caterham Valley.   F. J. Holbrook.

46. The Victorian villas next to 'The Hydro' and terraced 'Orchard Cottages' can be seen through the fence in Tupwood, which now borders the offices of Croudace Ltd. There were originally chalkpits on this corner of Tupwood Lane. 'Chalkpit Cottages', listed in the 1851 census, were demolished in 1971. In 1901 Caterham Gas Company, incorporated in 1869, planned to build gas holders on this site, but after a public enquiry the idea was abandoned.

White Nobs, Caterham Valley.

47. Victorian 'White Nobs House', standing between Godstone Road and Tillingdown Lane, was named after the farm in Godstone Road. An additional storey has been added to the house, now a service station by the Caterham by-pass. Tillingdown Lane leads to Tillingdown Farm, part of Tandridge parish until 1933 when it was transferred to Caterham and Warlingham Urban District.

Caterham, Timbers Hill.

48. 'Timber Hill Lodge', dated 1864, one of the first Victorian houses built after the railway was opened, has extensive views across the Valley from the front windows. The land in front was purchased by Caterham Urban District Council in 1900 from the Asprey family to provide a recreation ground for Valley children. The steps on the right led to a footpath to Tillingdown.

Caterham from Timber's Hill.   H. Grinstead.

49. Photographed from Crescent Road above the Police Station, Alchin's Livery Stables can be seen behind the 'Old Surrey Hounds'. St. John's Church tower is on the left and the Congregational clocktower in the centre. On the right, behind the coverway leading to the railway platform, is a clear view of 'The Priory' built next to the station for William Garland Soper in 1868. This postcard was published by Henry Grinstead, the Upper Caterham postmaster.

Mount Pleasant View, Caterham.

50. This view from the top of Mount Pleasant in the winter sweeps across the Valley to the spire of St. Mary's Church at the top of Church Hill and the adjoining cemetery. In front is 'Sylva House', built between Waller Lane and Stafford Road, but destroyed by enemy action in the Second World War. In front of 'Sylva House' is 'The Garlands' in Stafford Road (now L.M. Beasley & Co. Ltd.).

Published by
H.Grinstead
Post Office.Caterham. 10092.

High Street, Caterham Valley.

51. High Street, Caterham Valley was the unofficial name of the Croydon Road shopping area. Although many shops had been built on the right hand side, in 1913 there was still land between the buildings which has been developed since. On the right, high above the 'Old Surrey Hounds', are the small terraced houses, known as 'Paddy's Heaven', originally built for the railway workers.

Bus Terminus, Caterham Valley. Nº 8767.

52. At the Bus Terminus, picking up passengers, is an open top omnibus on route 59A to Camden Town via Croydon, Thornton Heath, Streatham and Westminster Bridge. Behind Grand Parade is St. John's Church tower, dedicated in June 1893. The 850 seat church, costing £16,000, had been built eleven years earlier in 1882. Two years later in 1884, St. John's was designated a separate parish. On the two floors above the International Stores, a linen shop at the corner of Mount Pleasant, was the Caterham Institute. Opened in 1902, it had spacious reading rooms, lending library, billiard room and a lady members' room. The building had been erected in 1880 for the Caterham Coffee Tavern Company whose shareholders included many local tradespeople.

Caterham Valley. Croydon Road

Braid's Series.

53. These Croydon Road shops had living quarters above for family and shop assistants. G.R. Hill, the boot and shoe shop, opened in 1902 and only closed in 1983. G.H. Jones, the fishmonger on the corner of Mount Pleasant, was established in 1887. According to a 1916 advertisement in the Caterham Directory, his winter speciality was cod liver oil. The three shops on the left were also built in 1887, as the bricks above the first floor windows are red, white and blue to commemorate Queen Victoria's Golden Jubilee. The shop on the far left is now occupied by Guy Hewett, the greengrocer, the oldest family business in the Valley. Started in 1879 at 103 Croydon Road, it moved to the present premises in 1919.

The Square, Caterham Valley.

54. The Square photographed from Godstone Road, looking towards Croydon Road. Kilby's Livery Stables is behind the fountain while beyond the telegraph pole is the 'Greyhound' public house. The fields on the hill are now gardens in Stafford Road. Ledgers, the stationers and newsagent on the left at 4 Godstone Road who published this card, has a splendid postcard display in its shop window.

55. The 'Capitol' Cinema next to the 'Greyhound' in the Croydon Road was opened on 6th October 1928 by Caterham Urban District Council Chairman Hugh Mitchell who declared that 'this was one of the most important events that had happened in Caterham since it became an Urban District Council'. The 800 ticket holders saw 'The Further Adventures of the Flag Lieutenant' starring Henry Edwards and Isabel Jeans and on the stage 'Fisher and Ariani', a solo violinist and Italian prima donna. An earlier venture in 1913 had been the 'Picture Palace' behind the 'Commonwealth Tavern' managed by the licensee, George Gammon.

Croydon Road, Caterham Valley

Braid's Series

56. Alec Braid, printer and stationer, editor of the 'Caterham Free Press' and 'Caterham Weekly Press' from 1898 to 1909, took this photograph of his business premises, 47 Croydon Road, in 1908. He published the annual Caterham Directory first appearing in 1901 and the Guide to Caterham in 1908 designed to encourage new residents and attract visitors. These were illustrated with his own photographs. At the end of the Croydon Road shops was the 'Greyhound' with St. John's Church tower in the distance.

57. The Cottage Hospital, at the corner of Croydon Road and Beechwood Gardens, costing £3,400, commemorated Queen Victoria's reign. It was opened with splendid ceremony by her daughter, Princess Christian of Schleswig-Holstein, on 3rd June 1903. The Valley was decorated with patriotic flags and bunting. The carved stone tablet recording the event was placed between first floor windows facing Croydon Road. The hospital had replaced a smaller building on the same site, opened in 1875. Although charges were made for patients' treatment according to their means, the hospital relied heavily on local subscriptions and donations. 'Hospital Saturday' became an annual event and collections were made at numerous local functions.

58. This postcard, 'Croydon Road and Beechlands', was listed by Alec Braid in an April 1905 advertisement in both the 'Caterham Weekly Press' and, surprisingly, in the rival newspaper, 'The Purley, Caterham & Oxted Gazette'. It was taken in 1905 at the top of Beechwood Road above the Board School, with its small steeple (now an Adult Education Centre). The grassy playing field was surrounded by trees. The headmaster's house is at the side of the school. In Croydon Road, opposite the school, the first floor of 'Florence Court' can be seen. Across the Valley, rising out of the trees, is 'Beechlands', the Asprey family home in Stafford Road.

Beechwood Road, Caterham Valley   A. J. Braid, Caterham Valley

59. This photograph was also taken by Alec Braid from the field by the side of 37 Beechwood Road, looking over the rooftops towards Manor Park. The large detached houses built on the Warlingham hillside can be seen in the distance above Whyteleafe Lime works.

BOURNE WATER AT CATERHAM VALLEY.

Braids Series

60. The Bourne water rose dramatically in February 1904 after heavy rains in 1903. There was serious flooding from 'Wapse's Lodge' along the valley to Purley and problems at the Kenley Waterworks. It was estimated that the flow was over seven million gallons a day. This phenomenon occurred every six or seven years and traditionally was said to herald a national disaster. This postcard is from a set of six photographs published by Alec Braid in a special illustrated supplement to the 'Caterham Weekly Press' on 5th March 1904. 'Bourne Water Picture Postcards' were advertised at one penny each or twopence each for real photographic views.

Wapse's Lodge, Caterham Valley.

61. 'Wapse's Lodge' stood at the junction of five roads – to Whyteleafe, Warlingham, Woldingham,
Caterham Valley and Coulsdon. The road to Whyteleafe can be seen here. The signpost on the left
points to Marden Park and Woldingham. In 1851 it was the first house in Caterham parish on the
Croydon-Eastbourne Road, standing near the 'Half Moon Inn', a coaching stop (now a garage).

The Slopes. Caterham

62. The Slopes dropped from Burntwood Lane to the railway line. As there was a footpath from Burntwood Lane to Tillingdown, crossing Stafford Road and Croydon Road, gates were installed each side of the railway line. The house on the right by the railway is 233 Croydon Road.

The Slopes. Caterham. 4

63. This is the same view of The Slopes after the Beechlands estate was sold in 1925. Houses were built in Stafford Road and higher up the hill in Milner Road. The Milner Close houses were later built each side of the footpath. This postcard was sent from 4 Milner Close. 'Our garden goes up to those trees. We have such a lovely view. I never saw such a view before,' was written on the reverse side.

COUNCIL OFFICES, CATERHAM

427

64. The Soper Memorial Hall was built to provide the Caterham Urban District Council with a Council chamber and offices and the town with a hall suitable for local functions. Before it was opened in January 1912, the Council met in the Masonic Hall, Stafford Road and council business was transacted from a room in Godstone Road. It was a memorial to William Garland Soper, who died in December 1908. A leading congregationalist, Justice of the Peace, first Chairman of Caterham Urban District Council in 1899 and County Alderman, he contributed generously in time and money to local activities. Costing £4,000, of which £1,500 was raised by public subscription, Soper Hall was designed by Henry Martin, the Council's surveyor. It was intended to add a Carnegie Library, but the proposal was defeated at a referendum held in 1912.

65. This aerial view shows the imposing Congregational Church, built in 1875 for £14,000 for the large and influential local congregation. Harestone Lecture Hall, behind the church, was opened on 4th June 1878 and on 5th August the clock made by Messrs. Gillet and Bland of Croydon for £252 was installed. On the right is the front garden of 'Beechwood'. Eothen School was opened in January 1892 in the centre of the three Victorian houses. Nos. 1 and 2 'West View', on the left, have been demolished and Eothen School assembly hall built in their place. 'Dalestead', on the right, is part of Tandridge District Council Offices.

Caterham, Congregational Church

66. Harestone Lecture Hall, on the right, with its small steeple, was used for meetings of the Harestone Literary Society, Caterham Institute and Caterham Debating Society. During the First World War it was quickly converted to Soldiers' Rooms for off duty guardsmen for in 1915 there were 15,000 recruits at the Guards' Depot. They could obtain hot meals, read newspapers, periodicals and books and write letters home. 'Beechwood', home of the Clarke family, keen congregationalists, is in the centre and 'Devon House' on the left. Built on Church Hill, with splendid views across the Valley, their drives were in Harestone Valley Road.

Caterham, Harestone Valley.

67. 'Harestone' was built by William Garland Soper in 1879 on land between Harestone Valley Road and Tupwood New Road (Harestone Hill). The entrance to this substantial mansion, with its attractive stable block (now converted to private homes), was in Colbourn Avenue. Originally a footpath, it was widened to a carriage drive when the house was built. The Hare Stone, now outside Caterham School, stood in its landscaped gardens.

68. The School for the Sons of Congregational Ministers, founded in 1811, moved from Lewisham to Caterham in October 1884 with 114 boarders. 'Withernden', a private school in Harestone Valley, was purchased, situated conveniently near the Congregational Church. Extensive additions were made and later 'Foxburrow', 'Shirley Goss' and 'Beechanger', whose roof can be seen in the bottom left hand corner, were purchased. Known locally as 'The College', it was renamed Caterham School in 1912. At the time of its centenary in 1984, it had over 700 pupils, the majority day boys, with girls admitted in the sixth form. The steep unmade road is Harestone Lane, formerly Pepper Alley, the short cut from the school to the Hill.

The Garden City, Caterham.

2196.   Ledger's Series.

69. The Garden City, at the end of Harestone Valley, was advertised in the 'Caterham Weekly Press' in 1907: *About 700 ft. above the sea, very beautiful plots of land for Cottages and Houses, of approved design only, for sale at War Coppice, with frontage to Woodland Way and Weald Way. Many plots are finely timbered. Exceedingly moderate prices.*

Caterham. A Path in the War Coppice.

70. 'A Path in the War Coppice' was one of Alec Braid's best selling postcards. The proximity of the Surrey Hills attracted new residents, visitors and day trippers in trains, brakes and on bicycles from London to Caterham. The 'Caterham Weekly Press' reported that on Easter Sunday and Monday 1901 over 1,400 passengers arrived at Caterham station by the South-Eastern Railway. War Coppice was reputed to be the site of an Iron Age hill fort and evidence has been found of Roman occupation.

THE VIEW AT VIEW POINT, CATERHAM.

71. The view at View Point near War Coppice was breathtaking and peaceful. Below the North Downs, on the left, tucked among the trees, is Godstone village. The patchwork of fields stretched to the South Downs, which can be seen on a fine day. Today, although the view is outstanding, the M25 motorway cuts across the fields and quarries have replaced farmland.

NO 16. VIEW FROM "WAR COPPICE" CATERHAM.

Bunce Bros
Langdale Studio
Caterham

72. The Water Tower, in War Coppice Road, dominates the skyline. Built in 1862, it is owned by the East Surrey Water Company. Since Bunce Bros. published this photograph, the view has changed as the grassy slopes are covered with trees.

73. The Sight Tower, White Hill, a folly built by Jeremiah Long, stands in a field opposite his residence, 'Arthur's Seat'. Although derelict now, it was possible to see the sea at Shoreham Gap from the top of the tower.

The Harrow Inn, Caterham.

74. 'The Harrow Inn' in Stanstead Road opposite Roffes Lane, the road to Chaldon village, was situated in the small hamlet of Stanstead. One of the oldest public houses in Caterham, it was listed as a beer house in the 1851 census. 'Lashmar Cottages', seen behind the hedge, now demolished, were believed to be the original inn, in some documents called 'The Arrow'.

75. 'Woodside' was one of several Victorian mansions situated in Stanstead Road with superb views over the Valley. This aerial view shows the back of the house, now demolished. Built in 1861 for Juland Danvers, a Caterham Railway director, it was successively occupied by the Street and Valentine families. Both families were interested in music and recitals were held in the fine music room. Bryan Valentine (1908-1983) was the Kent and England cricketer.

Stanstead Road, Upper Caterham.

76. This last photograph, appearing on a Frith postcard, was taken in Stanstead Road before the road was straightened, widened, made up and street lighting installed. It was part of an ancient highway leading from Bletchingley, up White Hill, through Platt Green, Stanstead hamlet, Stanstead Heath to the old village of Caterham and St. Lawrence's Church.